Visual ⊕ Expl

Global Warming

BARRON'S

All inquiries should be addressed to:
Barron's Educational Series, Inc.
250 Wireless Blvd.
Hauppauge, New York 11788
www.barronseduc.com

ISBN: 978-1-4380-1082-3
Library of Congress Control Number: 2017941029

Date of Manufacture: July 2017
Manufactured by: Toppan Leefung Printing Co., Ltd., Shenzhen, China

9 8 7 6 5 4 3 2 1

Photo credits:
Image credits: (t) top, (c) center, (b) bottom, (l) left, (r) right, FF (Fact file)

Alamy – p7 (bl) Alec Scresbrook. p15 (tl) Loop Images Ltd. p18 (main) Arterra Picture Library. p19 (tl) Justin Hoffman. p26 (main) ROPI. **European Marine Energy Centre Ltd** – p29 (tl) Mike Brookes-Roper/OpenHydro. **Flickr** – p15 (r) Jennifer Schlick. p19 (tr) Ken Yang. p21 (tl) Robert Oceans, (tr). p25 (bl) Larry Schwan. p27 (cl) Anderson Luis Schmidt. p28 (cl) Celisa B.M.Serra. p29 (br) Alejandro Flores. **Green Belt Movement** – p31 (cr). **Liter of Light** – p31 (br). **Shutterstock** – FC (main) Viktor Gagarin, (bl–br) Vadym Lavra, FloridaStock, Ammit Jack, Melih Cevdet Teksen. BC (tl) Phil MacD Photography, (br) Rawi Rochanavipart, Martin Metsemakers. p1 maradon 333. p2–3 James Whilock. p4 (main) Vadym Lavra, (br) Bradley L. Grant. p5 (tl) TZIDO SUN, (cl) Dan Bach Kristensen, (bl) ktsdesign, (tr–br) Ed-Ni Photo, kaband, Joseph Sohm. p6 (bl) Piotr Debowski, (main) Merydolla. p7 (cl) jose marques jopes. (tr–br) kram9, nounours, Viikramaditya Rai, Peter Kniez. p8 (main) Wead. p9 (tl) Ksenia Ragozina, (cl) Petri jauhianen, (tr–br) rck_953, The Pathetic Photographer, thechatat, Amazon-Images. p12 (b) GunnerL, (main) Accent Alaska.com. p13 (tl) bibiphoto, (cl–cr) Nahorski Pavel, E.G. Pors, Alexey Y. Petrov, (bl) GE_4530, (tr–br) Africa Studio, xpixel, vovan. p15 (bl) Zacarias Pereira de Mata, (tr) Meryll, (r) Digital Media Pro, (br) Bachkova Natalia. p16 (main) Doug McLean, (br) AlenaLitvin. p18 (br) Brais Seara. p19 (cl) Ethan Daniels, x, (cr) Davdeka. p20 (cl) TripDeeDee Photo, (main) Mircea C. p21 (rc) Steffen Foerster, Peter Schwarz. p22 (main) Chase Dekker, (cl) Andrey Shcherbukhin. p23 (tl) Gabor Kavacs Photography, (cl) D. Kucharski K. Kucharska. (bl) Ed Schneider, (cr) FotoRequest, (br) Brian Lasenby. p24 (main) Melih Cevdet Teksen, (br) Jannis Tobias Werner. p25 (tl) saiko3p, (cl) Matthew J Thomas, (tr–br) viennetta, x, costas anton dumitresco. p27 (tl) Rena Schild. p28 (main) Adellyne. p29 (cl) Teun van den Dries, (bl) nostal6ie. p30 (main) wavebreakmedia, (br) surajet.I. p31 (tr) SamJonah, VGstockstudiio. p32 (br) ktsdesign. **NASA** – p9 (tl) NASA/SDO. p11 (cl), (bl) JPL-Caltech, (br). p14 (main) ISS. p17 (tl–tc) JPL/NGA, (bl). p21 (bl). p21 (br) S. McKenzie Skiles, Snow Optics Laboratory, NASA/JPL. **NOAA** – p17 (cl), (tr–br). p19 (bl) Office of Ocean Exploration and Research. **Public domain – BC** (cr) Andreas Habich, p10 (bl), (main) Andreas Habich. p11 (tr–br). p15 (cl) US Marines. p19 (br). p25 (cl) US Air Force. p26 (br) UNFCCC. p27 (bl) World Health Day. p29 (cr) Derek Voller, Highways England. **Rainforest Connection** – p31 (tr). **Science Photo Library** – p14 (bl) British Antarctic Survey. p21 (cl) Bernard Edmaier. p23 (tr) Michael Durham/Minden Pictures. p31 (tl) Jim West. **Solar Roadways** – p29 (tr). **SunSawang** (solar panels) – p31 (br).

Introduction

Global warming is changing the planet we live on before our eyes. From unstable weather to unusual animal behavior, species loss, and disappearing islands, climate change has devastating consequences for humans and the natural world around us. Understanding the science behind what global warming is, how it is caused, and the impact it has on Earth is the only way we can come close to knowing the most important thing: what action we can take before it's too late.

Contents

Read on to learn about the global effects of climate change...

3

What is global warming?

Global warming is the **gradual** rise in the temperature of the Earth's atmosphere, which is the **envelope** of gases that **surrounds** our planet. This means that global warming affects the whole world and **every** living thing on it. Throughout Earth's 4.5-billion-year history, it has **experienced** many changes—ice ages followed by **warmer** periods—but the rate and causes of recent changes are **unique**. Since 1880, Earth's atmosphere has warmed by around **1.5° F** (0.8° C). By the close of the 21st century the **increase** could be 5–7° F (2–4° C).

Some predict that when a baby born today is 80 years old, Earth will be 7.2° F (4° C) warmer.

Facts and figures

What's the difference?

Global warming
Global warming is one aspect of climate change.

It is the long-term warming of the planet. The increases in temperature have been well documented in the 20th century.

Global warming is caused by the buildup of greenhouse gases in the Earth's atmosphere.

Climate change
Climate change encompasses global warming as well as other processes.

Climate change includes rising sea levels, shrinking glaciers, accelerating ice melt, changing long-term weather patterns, and variations in the length of seasons.

Climate change is a result of global warming.

Many of the world's largest rivers are drying up because of climate change

Real or...

Thousands and thousands of pages of research have been produced by many scientists that prove that current global warming is due in large part to human activity.

... a hoax?

There are many people, including many respected scientists, who believe that global warming is not proven or is not due to human activity.

Did you know?

Athabasca Glacier in the Canadian Rockies has shrunk 0.93 mi (1.5 km) in the last 125 years. The marker shows the extent of the glacier in 1908. In the distance is the glacier today.

As temperatures rise, rice releases extra greenhouse gas

Greenhouse gases

Some of these gases, like carbon dioxide and water vapor, occur naturally. Others are man-made, but methane has both natural and man-made sources.

Carbon dioxide (CO_2)
Excessive CO_2 is produced by burning fossil fuels. 1,102.3 US tons (1,000 metric tons) of CO_2 enter the atmosphere every second.

Methane (CH_4)
Intense agriculture, livestock farming, coal mining, and burning of natural gas have increased CH_4 concentration levels.

Chlorofluorocarbons (CFCs)
This type of synthetic refrigerant and aerosol gas was banned in 1996. It was proven to be destroying the ozone layer.

Causes in a nutshell

The changes on our planet are caused by natural events, like variations in the Sun's output and by volcanic activity, for example. They also result from the burning of fossil fuels, like coal, that are causing increases in the greenhouse gas emissions, which are trapped in the Earth's atmosphere.

The largest glacier on the Greenland ice sheet is melting

Effects in brief

The primary effect of greenhouse gas emissions is that they prevent heat from escaping Earth's atmosphere. This in turn affects the acidity of oceans, weather extremes, ozone depletion, temperature rises, ice melt, sea levels, alterations in ecosystems, human dislocation, and more.

What could happen?

Without emission-cutting action, by 2100 the Earth could warm by 7.2° F and oceans rise by 10–32 in. There would be extremes of hot or cold and countries with too much water or none at all. With no action and a 3.6° F (2° C) rise, oceans would submerge the homes of 280 million people.

To limit temperature rise to 3.6° F (2° C) means cutting emissions by half

Earth's natural cycles

The **Earth** is an ideal environment for living things because several processes keep it and its atmosphere in **perfect** balance. These processes are **natural** cycles that protect the Earth from receiving too much **radiation** from the Sun and provide water that is fit for drinking and air that is clean to breathe. All **life** on this planet depends on **cycles** working properly. Animals, including humans, and habitats can **adapt** to changes, but if changes to temperatures, **ocean** levels, and air and water quality are too large or happen too quickly, **adaptation** is unlikely.

Did you know?

Forests protect the planet by absorbing CO_2, but woodlands the size of Greece are being destroyed every year. This means more CO_2 is being released into the atmosphere.

The greenhouse gas layer is like a thermal blanket, but if the blanket is too thick, too much heat stays trapped under it

Earth is sometimes called the Goldilocks planet, because it is "just right."

Natural greenhouse

Natural levels of greenhouse gases ensure that Earth gets the right amount of the Sun's heat. Too much or too little of the gases would make Earth too hot or too cold.

Sun's radiation

The ideal temperature for Earth is 60.8° F (16° C). The greenhouse gas layer lets some radiation through; the rest is reflected back.

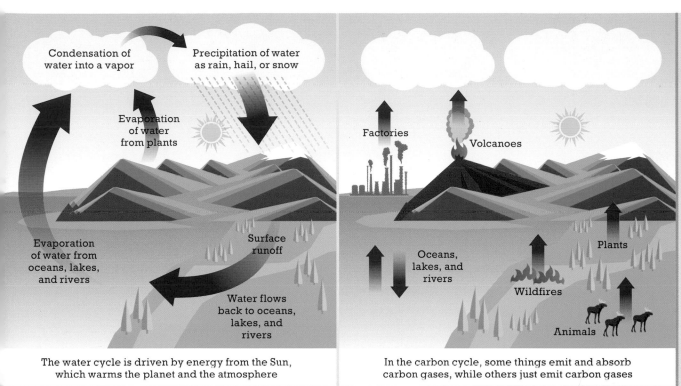

Condensation of water into a vapor

Precipitation of water as rain, hail, or snow

Evaporation of water from plants

Evaporation of water from oceans, lakes, and rivers

Surface runoff

Water flows back to oceans, lakes, and rivers

Factories

Volcanoes

Oceans, lakes, and rivers

Plants

Wildfires

Animals

The water cycle is driven by energy from the Sun, which warms the planet and the atmosphere

In the carbon cycle, some things emit and absorb carbon gases, while others just emit carbon gases

Some plants, like corn, absorb lots of CO_2 while growing

Water cycle

As Earth's temperature increases, more water is evaporated. The water vapor collects in the air, but as warmer air can hold extra vapor, it results in rainstorms and flooding in that region. This abnormal water cycle means that another region will be enduring drought conditions.

Carbon cycle

Carbon is in all living things and every part of the planet. Some things absorb carbon, while others release it. While this recycling is in balance, the carbon cycle works. When carbon-based fossil fuels are burned, CO_2 is released, with most of it ending up in the atmosphere and not in the carbon cycle.

Nitrogen cycle

This natural process is more out of balance than the carbon cycle. Burning fossil fuels and producing fertilizer for agriculture has produced an excess of nitrogen that is altering the normal nitrogen cycle. This change will have a negative effect on water quality, plant growth, human health, and global warming.

Nitrogen run-off from the fields has caused this bloom of harmful blue-green algae

Natural phenomena

Some **natural** events that occur on Earth and the Sun can cause changes in Earth's **atmosphere** and closer to home. These phenomena include **volcanic** eruptions, solar flares, natural release of methane and **ocean** evaporation, and climate events like **El Niño**. Each can increase temperatures and contribute to global warming, but their influence is too **small** to explain the dramatic **warming** of the planet over the past century. But as the temperature continues in an **upward** direction, the frequency of some of these natural **phenomena** will also increase.

Natural phenomena have occurred for millions of years, and will do so until the end of time.

Humankind's contribution to greenhouse gas emissions is 100 times that of volcanoes

Did you know?

Between 1650 and 1850, the northern hemisphere had a "Little Ice Age." It may have been caused by low solar radiation, increased volcanic activity, or changes in ocean currents.

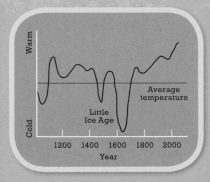

Methane in wetlands

During decomposition, plants and animals release methane, a greenhouse gas. As temperatures rise, some wetlands are releasing higher amounts of methane.

Carbon in oceans

Oceans store a lot of carbon, but with higher temperatures, evaporation rates increase to release more carbon as CO_2.

Volcanoes

All the world's land and undersea volcanoes spew around 220.5 million US tons of CO_2 per year (human-generated CO_2 per year is around 31 billion US tons into the atmosphere). This greenhouse gas can cause warmer temperatures, but some eruptions result in temperatures dropping.

Solar events

Solar flares and solar winds are energy surges on the Sun that can affect atmospheric conditions on Earth. These "storms" peak on an 11-year cycle. The Sun is slightly brighter now than it was 100 years ago, but solar events are thought to contribute minimally to global warming.

A solar flare erupts on the right-hand side of the Sun

Solar events exhibit themselves on Earth as colorful auroras

Ocean currents

El Niño events, which occur every 2–7 years, are when southern Pacific Ocean currents are disrupted. The 2014–2015 "super" El Niño, which caused abnormal rainstorms in the Americas and drought in Australia, contributed to record temperatures in 2016 and the release of extra CO_2.

The Atacama Desert, one of the world's driest places, flowers as El Niño brings rain

The greenhouse effect

Earth's **surface** temperature of 59° Fahrenheit (15° C) is regulated by greenhouse gases in the atmosphere, which **absorb** ultraviolet radiation from the **Sun**. Without these naturally-occurring gases, forming a **thermal** blanket around the Earth, the planet would **freeze**; with too much, it would heat up. Either way, life on Earth could not **survive**. Imagine the greenhouse layer is a gardener's greenhouse: the Sun **warms** the air inside the glass in the day, creating good conditions for plants to **grow**, but at night some of the heat is **released** back into the air to regulate the temperature.

Facts and figures

Top greenhouse gas emitters (2012) and % of total emissions		
China	24%	The top 10 emitting countries are responsible for over 70% of total emissions.
United States	12%	
European Union	9%	5 of the top 10 emitters are developing countries.
India	6%	
Russian Federation	5%	The lowest 100 emitting countries are responsible for less than 3% of total emissions.
Brazil	4%	
Indonesia	4%	
Japan	3%	
Canada	2%	
Mexico	1.5%	The energy industry is responsible for over 75% of total emissions.
(Source: World Resources Institute)		

Benxi, China, is a steel and coal town, and is the most polluted place on Earth, with dangerous levels of greenhouse gases

When a planet begins to warm up, it is hard to slow the process and almost impossible to stop it.

Did you know?

The first use of the term "greenhouse effect" appeared in a paper in 1909 by British scientist John Henry Poynting when he compared the atmosphere to a greenhouse.

What is ozone?

Ozone (O3) is a rare natural gas. "Good" ozone, found 6.2–10.6 mi (10–17 km) above Earth, absorbs damaging ultraviolet sunlight. "Bad" ozone on Earth's surface is found in smog.

Ozone damage

"Good" ozone–depleting gases, like man-made fluorocarbons (CFCs and HFCs), put holes in the Arctic and Antarctic ozone.

The Sun's rays enter the Earth's atmosphere

1

2

3 The greenhouse gases keep Earth's temperature to 59° F (15° C)

Some heat passes back out into space

Heat is emitted back from the Earth's surface

Some heat is absorbed by the greenhouse gases in Earth's atmosphere, which gets warmer

4

Venus is smothered by a cloud of CO_2

Greenhouse gases

The principal greenhouse gases in Earth's atmosphere are water vapor (H_2O), carbon dioxide (CO_2), methane (CH_4), nitrous oxide (N_2O), fluorinated gases (like CFCs, PFCs, and SF6), and ozone (O_3). They are all natural gases, and H_2O accounts for 95% of the greenhouse gases.

Fact file

Leading scientists

Hundreds have contributed to our knowledge of Earth's atmosphere. Those below represent four significant events along the way.

John Tyndall (d. 1893)

In 1824, this physicist demonstrated that gases in the atmosphere absorb heat in varying degrees.

Joseph Fourier (d. 1830)

In 1824, this French mathematician asked "What regulates the Earth's atmospheric temperature?"

Svante Arrehenius (d. 1927)

In 1896, this Swedish scientist proved that excess CO_2 would cause global warming.

James Hansen

In 2000, this climatologist made climate change a global issue when he spoke to the US Congress.

Too little, too much

Mars's thin atmosphere is mostly CO_2 with hardly any H_2O or ammonia (NH_3). This weak greenhouse effect results in a planet surface that is frozen. Venus has a runaway greenhouse effect with too much CO_2. Its surface temperature reaches 863.6° F (462° C), which is hot enough to melt lead.

Enhanced effect

Greenhouse gases in the correct amount maintain Earth's life-giving temperature, but in the enhanced greenhouse effect, too much CO_2 (from burning fossil fuels) enters the atmosphere, making the greenhouse layer thicker. This means more of the Sun's heat is trapped below, warming the planet.

Average CO_2 concentration November 21–December 27, 2014

The yellow and red areas show where CO_2 is above 397 parts per million (ppm).

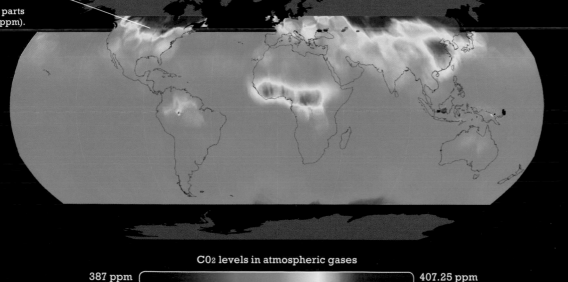

CO_2 levels in atmospheric gases

387 ppm

407.25 ppm

Fueling energy needs

Humans used wood—a renewable resource—as **fuel** until 1000 BCE, when it was supplanted by **coal**—a non-renewable fossil fuel. During the Industrial Revolution, starting in 1750, the **demand** for fossil fuels **exploded**. As living conditions improved, populations **increased**, fueling the need to extract even more fossil fuels. For 800,000 years before the 1800s, **CO2** in the atmosphere was 180–280 parts per million (ppm). Less than **200** years later, it is over 400 ppm. Currently, fossil fuels create 85% of global **energy**, with **15%** coming from nuclear, biofuel, biomass, wind, and solar energy.

Facts and figures

Global use of fossil fuel energy

Natural gas: a cube 5.6 mi (9 km) by 5.6 mi (9 km) by 5.6 mi (9 km) of natural gas used daily.

Coal: a pile of coal 258 yd (236 m) by 735 yd (672 m) used daily.

Oil: 96 million barrels of oil and liquid fuels used a day. A barrel is 42 gal (159 l). Every 15 seconds, an Olympic-size pool of oil is used.

Top fossil fuel users around the world

Natural gas: US uses about half a cubic mile (2 cubic km) a day.

Coal: China burns 11 million tons a day.

Oil: The US uses 19 million barrels a day.

Oman, Qatar, Kuwait, Saudi Arabia, and Brunei Darssalam rely on fossil fuels for almost all their energy.

Did you know?

In Hong Kong, air conditioners use 30–60% of all the electricity generated. Absorbing the CO2 emissions of one unit running for eight hours takes a mature tree three months.

There are about 500 offshore oil rigs in the world extracting nearly 90 million barrels of crude oil per day

CO2 record

The Mauna Loa Observatory in Hawaii takes daily readings of CO2 concentrations in its local atmosphere. The highest daily average was 409.44 ppm on April 9, 2016.

CO2 per person

Each person in the US produces 26.5 US tons (24 metric tons) of CO2 a year. This is equal to filling 12 hot air balloons with CO2 gas.

85% of our energy comes from fossil fuels— and it is increasing.

About fossil fuels

Natural gas, coal, and oil were formed 300 million years ago from the remains of dead organisms like trees, plants, and marine animals. Fossil fuels are a non-renewable resource, as they are being used up far faster than they can be formed. When burned, fossil fuels release energy and waste products.

A giant digger can excavate 264,555 US tons of coal a day

A car emits about 411 g of CO_2 per mile (1.6 km)

A super container ship uses 17.6 US tons of fuel/hour at sea

Airplanes emit 860 million US tons of CO_2 annually

Power generation contributes 25% of total CO_2 emissions

Combustion engine

The combustion engine, as used in vehicles and power stations, mixes fuel with air, then compresses and ignites it to release energy and exhaust gases. This means 1.2 billion cars, 20,000 planes, 62,500 power stations, and more emit greenhouse gases like CO_2 into the atmosphere every day.

What next?

Many experts in the energy sector predict that fossil fuel use will continue to rise over the next decades. Individual energy use is increasing, as is that of developing countries. Continued fossil fuel use means CO_2 in the atmosphere will increase, as will global warming.

Fact file

Types of fossil fuels

The burning of all fossil fuels affects Earth's atmosphere, with coal releasing the most CO_2 and natural gas releasing the least.

Crude oil

Extraction: pumped from under the ground or sea, or extracted from shale oil.
Uses: processed into oils and fuels and used in the manufacture of plastics, fertilizers, and pesticides.

Coal

Extraction: dug out from the Earth via deep-cut or surface mines.
Use: mostly as fuel for power stations. It emits the most CO_2 of all the fossil fuels.

Natural gas

Extraction: by onshore or offshore drilling down to gas deposits.
Uses: to produce heat or electricity, as a fuel, and to make plastics, fertilizers, and other chemicals.

Climate change and weather

Earth's climate has always **changed**. It has cooled and warmed up over the **millennia**. So, there's nothing new about climate change except that the **current** rate of changes in factors like temperature, rainfall, and wind **patterns** is unprecedented in **Earth's** history. This means the weather we experience is also changing rapidly. Some **regions** are getting heavier rain than normal, causing extreme floods. Others are inflicted with **record** temperatures or reduced **rain**, followed by drought. But as climate changes, it **affects** the seasons—some lengthen, others shorten.

Hurricanes may be more intense because of warmer ocean surface temperatures and higher sea levels

Mega-heatwaves, like that **which caused 10,000 deaths** in **Russia** in 2010, **will become more frequent.**

Did you know?

Scientists learn about Earth's climate and atmosphere over the last 800,000 years by studying ice cores that are drilled 1.86 mi (3 km) down into glaciers and ice sheets.

2100 forecast

The 1,300 scientists on the Intergovernmental Panel of Climate Change (IPCC) forecast that Earth will heat up by 7.2° F (4° C) if greenhouse gases are not cut.

Erratic changes

Natural global warming makes the Earth hotter or colder. Man-made global warming will make climate events unpredictable.

Changes in rainfall

In a warming world, places with good rainfall are likely to have increased rainfall. This is because higher temperatures result in more evaporation from land and sea, and since a warm atmosphere can hold more moisture, there's more rain. In the northeastern US, days of heavy rainfall have doubled over the last 50 years.

Flood-causing rainfall in Cumbria, UK, in 2015 broke all UK records

California had 1,000 more wildfires in 2014 than in previous years

Dry areas drier

While some areas will have increased rainfall, others will see less rain than ever before. With higher temperatures and increased evaporation, drylands, which already barely support 250 million people, will be further degraded so they cannot yield crops or support livestock.

Intense storms

Storms may decrease in frequency as part of climate change, but increase in strength. This is because more water vapor in the atmosphere will feed bigger storms. There is also ongoing research into evidence that ocean waves are growing in size and speed, possibly due to warm ocean temperatures.

Massive waves crash on the coast of Portugal in 2014

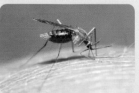

Changes in the oceans

About **70%** of the Earth's surface is covered with oceans. No wonder it is called the **"blue planet."** Though we name each ocean and sea, it is in reality one single, vast **body** of saltwater. Every form of life on Earth **depends** on the ocean for survival. It regulates climates; **absorbs** 95% of solar radiation; is integral to the water cycle; provides food for billions of **people**, and so much more. So, changes brought by global **warming** will have massive repercussions. If sea levels continue to **rise**, wetland ecosystems could inundate eight of the world's **largest** cities.

Facts and figures

All about ocean acidification

What is it?
It is a change in the chemistry of the ocean, making it more acidic.

What causes this?
Oceans absorb CO2, but with excess CO2 in the atmosphere, more is being absorbed by the oceans.

How is the acid made?
Seawater (H2O) and CO2 combine to make carbonic acid (H2CO3). This increases the ocean's acidity.

How acidic is the ocean?
For 300 million years, oceans had a pH of around 8.2, but since the 1800s, pH is 8.1.

What is affected?
Eventually every marine creature from plankton upward will be affected. Coral and shellfish are at especially high risk.

Rising sea levels flooded half the world's wetlands between 1970 and 2008.

Ice-free Arctic Ocean

Scientists believe the Arctic could be iceless in a few years—for the first time in 100,000 years. This would open the region to shipping and the extraction of oil and gas.

Opaque, dark water

In Norway, more rain and land runoff has meant that murky fjords are making coastal water opaque, blocking light for algae.

Did you know?

The melting of sea ice, which floats on the sea, does not increase sea levels. Ocean levels rise when ice held in glaciers, ice caps, ice sheets, and more melt.

Greater amounts of sediment are ending up in oceans as sea levels rise and land floods, or as droughts turn land to dust bowls

Rising sea levels

Since 1880, oceans have risen 7.9 in (20 cm) and are expected to rise by 11.8–39.4 in (30–100 cm) by 2100. Two causes are land ice melt and thermal expansion—when water expands (becomes less dense) when heated. The top 2,297 ft (700 m) of the ocean warmed by 1.8° F (1° C) over 50 years.

Calcifiers

As ocean acidity increases, carbonate ions decrease. This means that shell-building corals, plankton, and other marine creatures will find it harder to form calcium carbonate, the raw material for their shells. In addition, the shells of some animals have dissolved because of the increased acidity.

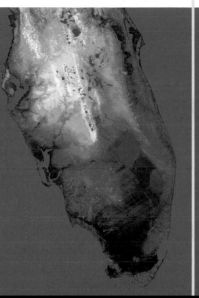

The green areas on this satellite image of Florida have low elevations

The pale blue shows areas that could be flooded by rising seas or a storm surge

An acidic ocean is starting to dissolve the shell of this sea snail

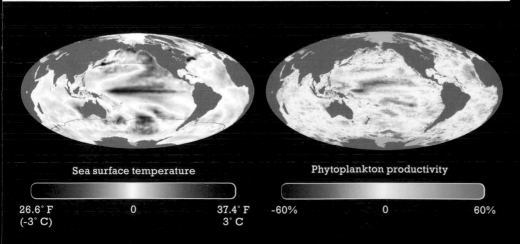

Fact file

Acidification timeline

The maps below show the increasing acidity of our oceans in 1875 and 1995, and forecasts for 2050 and 2095. For 300 million years, the oceans had a pH of 8.2, but over the last 200 years it has lowered to a pH of 8.1. This means that seawater is slightly less alkaline and slightly more acidic. Since pre-industrial times, CO_2 in the oceans has risen by 30%.

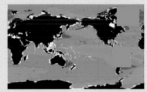

1875: pH 8.2

1995: pH 8.1

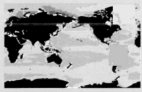

2050: pH 8

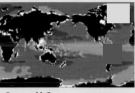

2095: pH 7.8

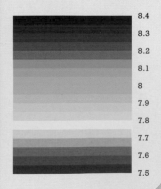

8.4
8.3
8.2
8.1
8
7.9
7.8
7.7
7.6
7.5

Ocean surface temperature and phytoplankton productivity between 2000 and 2004

Sea surface temperature

26.6° F (-3° C)   0   37.4° F 3° C

Phytoplankton productivity

-60%   0   60%

Critical phytoplankton

Phytoplankton use 100 million tons of CO_2 a day for photosynthesis, but phytoplankton blooms are declining. Ocean warming and acidification mean less surface nutrients, so phytoplankton move to deeper, cooler water, where less sunlight results in less photosynthesis and fewer blooms.

Plight of marine life

The temperature **increase** in oceans is only 1.8° F (1° C), but it is **enough** to jeopardize the survival of many marine animals. Marine environments **respond** to global warming more slowly than do land habitats, but the reaction is **more** severe. We see the **plight** of emaciated polar bears swimming between widely **separated** lumps of ice to hunt seals. At the other end of the food chain, a **warmer** ocean is a boon to zooplankton, but spells disaster for others. To adapt to changing oceans, species **migrate** or expand their territories. If they can't, it can mean **extinction**.

Facts and figures

93.4 %
The amount of total global warming that is entering oceans.

2.1%
The amount of total global warming that is affecting glaciers, ice caps and sheets, and sea ice.

2,297 ft (700 m)
The depth of ocean water most affected by warming and the depth at which most marine life thrives.

95%
How much of Earth's oceans are unexplored.

2.2 million
The number of animal species that live in the oceans.

43%
The reduction in the size of the Arctic polar ice cap over 30 years.

40%
The decrease in phytoplankton since 1950.

A bearded seal on an ice floe in Svalbard, Norway, where temperatures in 2016 were 13.5° F (7.5° C) above average

If **Earth** continues **warming**, up to a **quarter** of all **plants** and **animals** could **become extinct** within **100 years**.

Did you know?

As cold-water fish species migrate to cooler water from warming water, it will affect seabirds like puffins and auklets. They will either follow the food or breed less.

Seaweed growth

Melting sea ice in Antarctica and the Arctic allows more sunlight to reach the sea floor. This encourages seaweed growth to the detriment of sponges and worms.

Adélie penguins

The population of breeding pairs of Adélie penguins in Antarctica has shrunk to 11,000. Thirty years ago there were 32,000.

As krill lose their sea-ice habitats, their numbers will fall and disrupt all food chains

Antarctic krill

Tiny krill are the main food source for the giants of the oceans—whales—and for penguins, seals, and fish. Increasing ocean temperatures and loss of sea ice will reduce the successful hatching and development of the larvae that feed on the algae that grows on the underside of sea ice.

Coral bleaching

Even a small change in temperature and ocean chemistry will adversely affect coral. Under heat stress, coral expels the algae that gives coral its colors, leaving the coral white. Bleached coral grows slowly (its energy comes from the algae) and is more likely to become diseased.

Coral bleaching killed a quarter of Australia's Great Barrier Reef in 2015–2016

Dependent on ice

Polar bears hunt both on and from ice for seals and other marine animals, but with ice melting earlier and faster, the hunting season has been cut by 30 days. Undernourished females are also producing fewer cubs. For bears that do breed, warming causes the ice caves that shelter the young to collapse.

A shorter hunting season means polar bears are 68–99 lbs (31–45 kg) lighter

Changes to the land

Global warming and climate change have wreaked their **greatest havoc** on the Antarctic, Arctic, Alaska, and northern regions of Canada and Russia, but **evidence** is all around in the form of changing **landforms** and habitats and shifting or disappearing resources, and in the frequency or intensity of **natural** events. Most serious is the **declining** freshwater resources that will impact **ecosystems** and more. For example, in Los Alamos, Mexico, in 2002–2003, **drought** pushed drought-resistant piñon pines too far, so they **fell** prey to bark beetles. Nine in every ten pines died.

Facts and figures

Effects of climate change on lakes and rivers

Reduced population
Salmon numbers have decreased because frequent, intense spring floods are washing away the eggs.

Dead zones
The process that adds oxygen to water slows with rising temperatures, creating dead zones of toxic algal blooms or foul drinking water.

Species on the move
As water temperatures rise, especially in shallow water, cold-water species will migrate or fail to breed while warm-water species will move in.

Low stream flow
Reduced stream flows can be just as dangerous for wildlife as flooding. Trout on their spawning run are more easily caught in shallow water by bears.

Did you know?

Known as "reservoirs in the sky," the mountain glaciers of the Himalayas are shrinking rapidly, and therefore reducing the water that feeds all of Asia's major rivers.

Rising temperatures affect how sugar maple trees photosynthesize, reducing their sugar sap

Altered woodlands

As habitats are affected by climate change, some saplings will fail to grow while others will only survive in limited areas.

More poison ivy

Increased concentrations of CO_2 in the warming air is good news for poison ivy—it is thriving. But it is bad news for the 80% of the population allergic to this noxious plant.

Because trees are so long-lived— from 40 to 5,000 years— the effects of climate change may go unnoticed for many years.

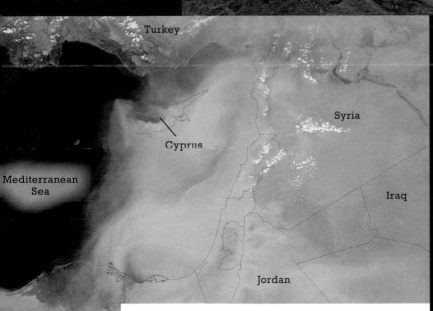

Three-quarters of the Maldives could be underwater by 2100

Hit by global warming

The catastrophic effects of our changing Earth can be witnessed in many places. Below are four locations and the problems faced.

Sudan, northern Africa
Desertification and reduced rainfall is causing a food crisis and tribal conflicts over fertile land.

Bolivia, South America
An 18,000-year-old glacier that provided water to 2 million people in La Paz has completely dried up.

The Alps, Europe
40% of Europe's freshwater is in the Alps, but disruption of the water cycle threatens disaster.

The Rockies, Colorado
Airborne dust and carbon darkens ice, making it absorb more energy from the Sun so it melts faster.

Disappearing islands

In 2016, it was announced that five of the Solomon Islands in the Pacific Ocean had disappeared under seas that had risen by 7.9 in (20 cm) over the previous 20 years. Rising sea levels are a result of thermal expansion and increased ice melt. Other island states like Kiribati also face this crisis.

Lakes and rivers form by melting permafrost in Siberia, Russia

Permafrost melt

Global warming has had its greatest impact on the world's coldest places, causing the permafrost—a 656–2,133 ft (200–650 m) layer of sub −32° F frozen soil—to melt. With the thaw, land collapses under forests and towns, and the CO_2 that had been stored in the soil is released into the atmosphere.

Desertification

When fertile land becomes arid, it is known as desertification. It is caused mainly by drought (a symptom of climate change) and the clearing of forests (deforestation). Another cause is bad agricultural practices. Desertification results in erosion, famine, and extinctions and adds to global warming.

In September 2015, a human-caused dust storm engulfed populated areas of the Middle East and North Africa

Effect on land animals

The first **animals** to feel the effects of climate change are those that thrive in **cold** temperatures. But in the effort to outrun rising temperatures, animals may be abandoning the **sources** of food and breeding sites of their **natural** habitats. In their new homes, they could face new **predators**, less food, or disease. Scientists **predict** that only 4% of animals and plants are likely to benefit from climate change; the rest will either **migrate** or become **extinct**. In 2009, the Bramble Cay melomys, a rodent, was the first mammal confirmed extinct as a result of climate **change**.

Facts and figures

Unexpected effects of global warming

More methane
The global livestock herd emits—via burps and manure—more methane than the oil and gas industry.

Farther to fly
The ivory gull nests on rocky cliffs and flies to sea ice to hunt. But retreating ice means farther to fly, less successful hunting, and less breeding.

No deep snow
Wolverines need dens for their young to be dug into deep snow for warmth and protection. Such sites will be reduced with rising temperatures.

Sex change
Bearded dragons are undergoing sex changes as a result of hot temperatures in Australia. Their sex is being determined by heat instead of chromosomes.

Did you know?

Alpine goats (chamois) have lost a quarter of their body mass since the 1980s. Rising temperatures mean that the goats are lazing about rather than foraging for food.

Some bears and cubs are ending hibernation 30 days earlier than usual because of rising temperatures

Climate changes will initiate a chain reaction of ecological effects.

Ant invader

Global warming could kill off the big-headed ant, the world's most invasive species. Climate change will affect its range.

Desert microbes

US research has shown that some bacteria that help bind the biocrust (top layer) of desert soil are dying because of warmer temperatures. Unanchored sand means more dust storms.

A koala returns to a eucalyptus forest that has regrown after a bush fire

Koala warning

Australian koala numbers are already affected by disease, forest die-back and clearing, pesticides, and bush fires. The increased frequency of bush fires and drought, caused by climate change, is expected to hit the existing population of 45,000–90,000 wild koalas very hard.

Fact file

Climate effects and mammals

The three mammals featured here demonstrate how some animals may successfully adapt, or not, to changes in climate.

Indiana bat
In response to climate change, this bat found new hibernation sites but also encountered a fatal fungal disease.

Snowshoe hare
To avoid being an easily-spotted meal, this hare needs its brown spring coat to arrive with the now-early snowmelt.

American pika
A factor that causes pika decline is being unable to find cooler temperatures no matter how high they head into the mountains.

Beetle outbreaks

When a spruce forest is weakened by disease or drought or is decimated by storms, it becomes subject to a beetle outbreak. Beetle numbers increase with the availability of dying or dead trees and benefit from the rising temperatures. These beetles have wiped out millions of acres of spruce forests around the world.

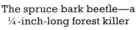

The spruce bark beetle—a ¼-inch-long forest killer

Raptors react

The rough-legged hawk has cut its winter migration by 186 mi (300 km) in response to climate change or changes in the movement of their prey. Other raptors, like the golden eagle, have shortened their migrations by just a few miles.

A rough-legged hawk in flight

Human consequences

Natural **disasters** have cost human lives throughout history. The Yangtze River **flood** in China in 1931 caused 3.7 million deaths from **drowning** and starvation, but there is a prediction of 100 **million** deaths by 2030 if global warming and climate change continue unchallenged. **90%** of those deaths will happen in developing **countries**, which are often those with the lowest CO2 emissions and the poorest communities. **Humans** need oxygen (air), water, food, shelter, and sleep to **survive**, and it is these things that climate change will **destroy**.

Facts and figures

Top five countries at most extreme risk from climate change (2014)

Bangladesh, Asia
Prone to floods and cyclones, with increasing problems resulting from higher rainfall and sea levels.

and heavy rainfall extremes, made worse by vast deforestation.

Haiti, Caribbean
Droughts cause crop failures and erosion, while deforestation worsens flood effects.

Guinea-Bissau, Africa
Flooding erosion causes food and water insecurity.

South Sudan, Africa
Unpredictable rainfall, desertification, and erosion result in food and water shortages.

Sierra Leone, Africa
Crops and water supplies are jeopardized by drought

Loss of fresh water

Sea level rises, especially in low-lying coastal areas, result in the contamination of groundwater drinking supplies by saltwater.

After 30 years of drought, only a third of Ethiopians have access to safe drinking water

Africa and South Asia— home to a third of the world's population— are most exposed to climate change.

Air quality

Excess CO2 and other pollutants in the air are reducing the quality of breathable air, causing respiratory diseases and the early death of 7 million people annually.

Did you know?

Lower Manhattan, New York, in darkness after Hurricane Sandy in 2012 caused a power failure. Storms of increasing intensity are likely to cause more-frequent grid collapses.

Taps run dry for up to 60 hours at a time in La Paz, Bolivia

Lack of water

La Paz, Bolivia, is likely to be the first capital city in the world to be largely abandoned due to the lack of fresh water, since its supply of glacial meltwater has dramatically reduced. Fresh water is going to become the world's most valuable resource. Death and conflicts will result.

Economic loss

In addition to loss of life, weather extremes cause billions of dollars worth of damage and can disrupt product and food production, resulting in a loss of income for many families. It may also cause people to move to safer regions, placing added stress on refuge cities and towns.

Fact file

Other effects

A disruption in a natural cycle is like a stone thrown into water—the ripples will radiate out to affect many aspects of human life for many years.

Cultures lost
Lack of rain caused Moroccan Berbers, in Africa, to abandon villages and ancient ways of life.

Escaping conflict
Some 2.3 million people have fled Sudan's civil war, which was caused, in part, by lack of water resources.

Less agriculture
Desertification in Kenya, Africa, means fewer crops and cattle, and therefore less produce for cities.

Long-lasting legacy
Lingering effects of Haiti's 2010 earthquake include tent cities, poor sanitation, and diseases like cholera.

In Skipsea, UK, 59 ft (18 m) of coastline were lost in a year due to bad storms

Crop failures

Climate change causes unpredictable extremes— too much or too little water and too high or too low temperatures— which reduce crop yield or destroy a crop completely. High concentrations of CO_2 result in lower nutrient levels in some grains, like wheat.

Corn damaged from drought in Kansas

What is being done?

There is **tireless** work happening around the globe to stem the causes and **effects** of climate change. The task is huge and requires individuals, industries, **manufacturers**, energy providers, **world** leaders, and governments to make significant changes, often against strong **resistance**. Tackling global warming requires information based on **thorough** research; lobbying by environmental groups and **individuals**; improvements in technology, making laws that **lower** greenhouse **gas** emissions, and that the commitment to change becomes action.

Facts and figures

What is carbon neutral?
When the amount of carbon emitted equals the same as the carbon replaced by renewable energy, offset by tree planting, or stored

Carbon-neutral places:
Vatican City, Italy; Ta'u, South Pacific; Samsø Island, Denmark.

Places pledged to be carbon-neutral:
British Columbia, province of Canada;

Copenhagen, capital of Denmark; Costa Rica, Central America; Iceland, Europe; the Maldives, South Asia; Norway, Europe; Tuvalu, South Pacific; and Sweden, Europe.

What is carbon negative?
When more carbon is absorbed than is emitted.

Carbon negative countries:
Bhutan, South Asia.

Carbon negative

Bhutan, South Asia, is carbon negative. Its forests absorb four times more carbon than the country emits. Its next aims are to grow 100% organic food and reduce waste to zero.

The **change** to a low-carbon economy will be **harder** if the **world waits** for a **climate crisis.**

A hall alongside St Peter's in carbon-neutral Vatican City is covered with 2,400 solar panels

World action

World Environment Day, started by the United Nations (UN), is June 5. It promotes awareness of environmental issues.

Did you know?

Governments, non-governmental organizations (NGOs), scientists, and environmental groups meet at summits to work out solutions to man-made global warming.

Earth Day

In 1970, Gaylord Nelson, a US senator, organized the first Earth Day after seeing the damage caused by a massive oil spill. Celebrated on April 22 each year, it urges people to make small changes to their way of life in order to clean up and protect our planet and its resources.

Vital research

Thousands of scientists are studying every aspect of global warming and climate change. Some are monitoring continents like the Arctic; others are focusing on a single plant or animal. All research is vital, as the results tell us what action needs to be taken and when, where, and how.

People join marches to influence governments and industries

This plane collects data on retreating sea ice, glaciers, and greenhouse gases in the Arctic

By 2030, 90 million people in Africa will be at risk of mosquito-borne malaria

Protecting health

To protect people's health from the effects of climate change, the World Health Organization (WHO) runs projects in 40 countries. Though some diseases may be reduced by climate change, most will increase. Malaria, for example, will spread with rising temperatures to more populated higher altitudes.

Reducing greenhouse gases

Even if the world stopped emitting **greenhouse** gases today, the planet would continue to **warm** for hundreds of years. Banning fossil fuels is not realistic, but it is realistic to **reduce** reliance on fossil fuels, **increase** use of renewable energy like solar or wind, find **new** types of clean energy, and increase Earth's capacity to store CO_2. There are **many** innovations in development; some are **undergoing** real-world testing. In Spain, the world's first **solar** towers power 94,000 homes, which **eliminates** 125,663 US tons (114,000 metric tons) of CO_2 annually.

Facts and figures

Ways of storing CO2

Plant forests
Trees absorb carbon, but we are losing about 10 billion trees each year, so less carbon is being absorbed. To impact carbon levels, it is estimated that 1 trillion more trees are needed. To date, UNEP and Plant for the Planet have planted 14 billion trees. China's "Great Green Wall" is a mission to plant 100 billion trees by 2050.

Offsetting carbon
Countries, companies, and individuals can buy into carbon-storing projects, like carbon forests, to counter their carbon footprint. This is carbon offsetting.

Carbon sequestration
This is when carbon is captured from power plants or industry and injected a half mile into the Earth. This carbon-storage technology is still in development.

Did you know?

Nuclear power has low emissions but its fuel—uranium—is rare, and issues about its safety have come to the fore after Japan's Fukushima plant was damaged by a tsunami in 2011.

Geothermal energy emits less than 5% of the CO2 emitted by a coal-fired power plant.

An Icelandic geothermal power plant using Earth's core temperature to heat water, which turns a steam turbine to make electricity

Lower emissions

To cut emissions and save fuel, planes may descend to land with engines idling, taxi on one engine, or take off at a steep angle.

Solar power

In 2014, solar power for 29 million homes was generated. This equates to one home in 52 globally. But on Ta'u, in the South Pacific, everything is solar powered!

Wave and tidal power

Harnessing the power of waves or tides to make energy is underused, but in 2000 the world's first commercial wave power station was installed off Islay, Scotland, generating electricity for 300 homes. Tidal power, which is more developed, is used in power stations in France and the United States.

This turbine uses tidal energy to generate electricity

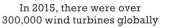

In 2015, there were over 300,000 wind turbines globally

Wind power

One offshore wind turbine can power 5,500 homes, and in Spain the wind farms power 10 million households. But still, wind power represents only 3.7% of global electricity supply. Imagine how much greenhouse gas could be removed from the atmosphere if that percentage increased?

Biomass energy

This energy comes from human, plant, and animal waste. Methane gas that can power a generator is released by rotting rubbish and when grasses, manure, and urine rot in a biodigestor. Burning waste wood trimmings that would otherwise be discarded is also a form of biomass energy.

Piles of wood trimmings at a biomass power plant

What you can do

Global warming and climate change are **massive** problems, but even **small** changes made by individuals, households, or communities will make a difference. Every day, the **majority** of the world's population uses too much **energy**—for transport, **heating** or cooling, lighting, hygiene, cooking, and in the products we **consume**, buy, and often throw away. There are schemes in action in many developing **countries** that are making inroads into deforestation and **clean** energy, and creating communities that **protect** their environment rather than harm it.

Reducing fossil fuel use and CO2 in the atmosphere will be achieved by big energy schemes and by individuals making small changes

Energy efficiency is the easiest, **quickest,** and **cheapest way** to reduce fossil fuel use.

Did you know?

Turning televisions, computers, and screens off rather than leaving them on standby could lower electricity use by 9–16% and save money on power bills at the same time!

Carbon footprint

There are many online sites (search: "carbon footprint calculator") where you can work out how much carbon you are emitting.

Phone chargers

A phone can be charged in just under two hours using a basic, inexpensive, mobile solar charger. Mobile chargers are pocket-sized and use UV rays, so it does not matter if it is overcast.

Recycling works

Recycling takes many forms, but all forms save energy. The recovery of methane to power generators is recycling our waste in the same way as paper products, bottles, cans, and more are recycled. It takes only six weeks for an aluminum can to be recycled and back on the shelves of stores.

A well dug into a landfill recovers methane gas usable for electricity

Smart energy meters monitor energy usage in the home

Energy smart

Smart meters have made it possible to monitor how much energy—gas and electricity—is being used in the home or office. They will pinpoint appliances that are inefficient and let householders see improvements in their energy use.

Precious water

The quantity of the world's drinking water is threatened by climate change. In 2009, 45 American states experienced water shortages. Using less water, specifically in Western households and in industry and agriculture, is as important as saving energy. Western homes are using six times the amount of water as an African family.

Save 1.6 gal (6 l) of water a minute by turning off the tap while washing up

Glossary

Adapt
The way in which an organism becomes more suited to its environment.

Algae
A single or multi-celled organism that has no roots, stems, or leaves and is often found in water.

Aurora
The phenomenon of the appearance of lights in the sky, especially around the northern and southern magnetic poles.

Biomass
Organic matter that can be used as fuel.

Calcifiers
Something that causes another thing to become hard or bony.

Carbon footprint
The amount of CO2 emitted Into the atmosphere due to the activities of an individual, organization, or community's activities.

Carbon negative
When more carbon is absorbed than is emitted (e.g., by a country's industrial activities) .

Carbon neutral
When the amount of carbon emitted (e.g., by a country's industrial activities) equals the same amount as the carbon replaced by renewable energy, or that which is absorbed by planted trees.

Carbon offsetting
A means of countering the effects of a carbon footprint.

Carbon sequestration
A relatively new form of carbon-storage technology, where CO2 is removed from the atmosphere and stored in liquid or solid form.

Carnivore
An animal that feeds on other animals—a meat-eater.

Chlorofluorocarbons (CFCs)
Gases typically used in refrigerants and aerosols that are harmful to the ozone layer.

Climatologist
Scientist who studies the Earth's climate.

Condensation
The process by which water changes from a gas to a liquid.

Decomposer
An organism, such as a bacteria or fungus, that consumes dead matter and returns it to ecological cycles.

Decomposition
Another word for "decaying" or "rotting," where a substance is broken down into a simpler form.

Deforestation
The clearing of a large area of trees.

Desertification
The action of fertile land being transformed into desert, usually due to such things as drought or deforestation.

Displacement
Humans or animals being forced to move from one place to another.

Ecosystem
A community of plants or animals and the environment to which they are adapted.

Evaporation
The process by which water turns from liquid to vapor.

Fossil fuel
A natural fuel (such as coal or gas) that has formed from plant or animal remains.

Germinate
A term used to describe when something begins to grow, such as a seed.

Greenhouse effect
Trapping of the Sun's heat in a planet's atmosphere.

Herbivore
A plant-eater.

Livestock
Farm animals that are used as assets.

Ozone layer
A layer in Earth's atmosphere that contains large amounts of ozone.

Parts per million (PPM)
A measurement based on concentration—such as the amount of CO2 in the atmosphere.

Photosynthesis
A chemical process that allows organisms to capture energy in sunlight and convert it into food.

Phytoplankton
Microscopic plants that live in the ocean and form the plant components of plankton.

Precipitation
The fall of water, ice, or snow from the atmosphere.

Radiation
Energy that moves from one location to another, leaving an object in the form of waves. Light, sound, and heat are examples of types of radiation. Many forms of radiation are dangerous.

Solar radiation
Radiation emitted from the Sun (see "Radiation" definition).

Solar wind
A stream of particles emitted by the Sun.

Trace gases
The gases that make up only a small proportion of our atmosphere, such as argon.

Index